IRISH FAVORITES

CONTENTS

HOW TO USE THE CD ACCOMPANIMENT:

THE CD IS PLAYABLE ON ANY CD PLAYER, AND IS ALSO ENHANCED SO MAC AND PC USERS CAN ADJUST THE RECORDING TO ANY TEMPO WITHOUT CHANGING THE PITCH.

A MELODY CUE APPEARS ON THE RIGHT CHANNEL ONLY. IF YOUR CD PLAYER HAS A BALANCE ADJUSTMENT, YOU CAN ADJUST THE VOLUME OF THE MELODY BY TURNING DOWN THE RIGHT CHANNEL.

ISBN 978-1-4234-9529-1

HAL•LEONARD® CORPORATION

7777 W. BLUEMOUND RD. P.O. BOX 13819 MILWAUKEE, WI 53213

Visit Hal Leonard Online at
www.halleonard.com

① BELIEVE ME, IF ALL THOSE ENDEARING YOUNG CHARMS

HORN

Words and Music by
THOMAS MOORE

❷ THE BELLS OF ST. MARY'S

HORN

Words by DOUGLAS FURBER
Music by A. EMMETT ADAMS

◆ BLACK VELVET BAND

HORN

Traditional

◆ BRENNAN ON THE MOOR

HORN

Traditional

◆5 COCKLES AND MUSSELS
(Molly Malone)

HORN

Traditional

◆ THE CROPPY BOY

Horn

18th Century Irish Folksong

◆7 DANNY BOY

HORN

Words by FREDERICK EDWARD WEATHERLY
Traditional Irish Folk Melody

◆ EASY AND SLOW

HORN

Traditional

◆9 THE FOGGY DEW

HORN

Traditional

🔟 GREEN GROW THE RUSHES, O

HORN

Traditional

🔶11 THE HUMOUR IS ON ME NOW

HORN

Traditional

I ONCE LOVED A LASS

HORN

Traditional

13 I'LL TAKE YOU HOME AGAIN, KATHLEEN

HORN

Words and Music by
THOMAS WESTENDORF

◆14 I'LL TELL ME MA

HORN

Traditional

🔶15 THE IRISH ROVER

HORN

Traditional

THE JOLLY BEGGARMAN

HORN

Traditional

17 THE LITTLE BEGGARMAN

HORN

Traditional

◆18 MacNAMARA'S BAND

HORN

Words by JOHN J. STAMFORD
Music by SHAMUS O'CONNOR

◆19 MINSTREL BOY

HORN

Traditional

20 MY WILD IRISH ROSE

Horn

Words and Music by
CHAUNCEY OLCOTT

◆21 A NATION ONCE AGAIN

Horn

Words and Music by
THOMAS DAVIS

❖22 THE OLD ORANGE FLUTE

HORN

Traditional

23 THE PATRIOT GAME

HORN

Traditional

Moderately

◆ 24 RED IS THE ROSE

HORN

Irish Folksong

◆25 THE RISING OF THE MOON

HORN

Traditional

THE ROSE OF TRALEE

HORN

Words by C. MORDAUNT SPENCER
Music by CHARLES W. GLOVER

◆ 27 TOO-RA-LOO-RA-LOO-RAL
(That's an Irish Lullabye)

HORN

Words and Music by
JAMES R. SHANNON

28 THE WEARING OF THE GREEN

HORN

18th Century Irish Folksong

WHEN IRISH EYES ARE SMILING

HORN

Words by CHAUNCEY OLCOTT
and GEORGE GRAFF, JR.
Music by ERNEST R. BALL

Moderately

◆30 THE WILD COLONIAL BOY

HORN

Traditional

31 ◆ WILD ROVER

HORN

Traditional